Becoming Me!

Being Myself

Getting Along with others

Taking Authority

and

Keeping the Faith

By

Dr. Derrick L. Randolph Sr.

Copyrighted Material

ISBN-13: 978-1-944166-11-3

ISBN-10: 1-944166-11-4

Introduction

To help us discover who we are becoming, we're going to learn from the stories of Jesus found in the gospel of Matthew. Matthew was a disciple called by God to follow the Lord Jesus Christ. Jesus called Matthew to follow Him, when Matthew was a tax collector. He collected ""toll" or "transport" taxes from Jewish merchants, farmers and caravans as they were passing through Galilee. Tax collectors were often criticized for collecting more taxes than were necessary and for growing wealthy on the extra "profits." These practices left Matthew disliked by other Jews. Since his job was to profit off of his fellow Jews, he would be treated like an outsider by the rest of his Jewish community. The good news is that by following Jesus, Matthew had the opportunity to finally become the man God intended him to be. Matthew could finally find his place in the community and find fulfillment in life. We will read through portions of the gospel that Matthew wrote and follow Jesus Christ, the man from Galilee who was rejected and despised by men. We will learn how to discover our own identity, develop the ability to get along with others, learn to take authority and maintain our faith in Jesus Christ. Let's watch Jesus.

Scenario

As we look at the lessons in the gospel of Matthew, we will apply them to a variety of scenarios. When you walk into a new setting like a classroom, neighborhood, or sports team, you may experience emotions of nervousness, fear, or anxiety. This may cause you to believe that you are shy, antisocial, insecure, introverted, or timid. Regardless of what you think about yourself today or what you are feeling inside when you are around others, you will benefit from the following lessons. You will get better at being yourself. Get prepared for the journey and join me as we become ourselves right in the midst of the crowd.

You will find the following components in each lesson:

- 'The Background Story' gives information about the Bible Story or situation that Jesus was in.

- 'The Bible Story' from the NIV version of the bible

- 'The Good News', a word of encouragement and hope

- 'The Truth' which is the main point of the lesson

- 'Agreeing with God' which is our personal commitment

- 'Text, Tweet, Tag or Post This' are social media posts

- 'Let's get to work' helps you start looking at your life

Read and sign the Agreement with God if you agree and commit to overcoming the obstacles in your path. Sometimes our obstacles are the way we look at our situation. Sometimes, obstacles are the way we feel about the difficult people in the crowd that we have to face. Sometimes they are the feelings of hesitance, fear of the unknown, or lack of confidence in ourselves.

Whatever our obstacles are, we will overcome them together. Remember that "we are more than conquerors through him who loved us." (Romans 8:31a) Nothing "will be able to separate us from the love of God that is in Christ Jesus our Lord." (Romans 8:39b)

Part 1 - Discovering Who I am

(Before I Face the Crowd)

One of the biggest discoveries that we experience when we are growing up is that we don't have the self-confidence that others have. If only we believed in ourselves, things would be different. If somehow we became content with who we were and with who we would one day become then life would have been a little easier for us. Then if we could somehow discover what we're supposed do in life, life would become really easy. Well, the bible gives us clues that will help us make these discoveries. We will learn about them for ourselves and yes, life will become easier.

One of the clues to finding this mysterious contentment is in finding my identity. I urge you to find out who you are, who you belong to and what God's plan is for you. Accepting these true statements about yourself will give you confidence and it will help you please God. Then you will be able to soar through life simply being yourself.

Through each phase of life, you will become a better person and get better in fulfilling your purpose. It all starts with you though. If you are willing to start out by being yourself, then you are on the road to becoming a better you. If you commit to improving your character and behaviors, life gets even more fulfilling. If you learn to handle life's situations God's way, then life becomes satisfying. It becomes fun.

Goal #1 - Being Myself

The Background Story

Jesus was special. He had a specific purpose in life. God had a plan for his life. According to this plan, Jesus had to go through a lot. Jesus' parents also had to go through a lot before Jesus was even born. In fact, Jesus's parents had to take him to Egypt to escape Herod's attempt to kill Jesus.

The Bible Story

When they had gone, an angel of the Lord appeared to Joseph in a dream. "Get up," he said, "take the child and his mother and escape to Egypt. Stay there until I tell you, for Herod is going to search for the child to kill him." So he got up, took the child and his mother during the night and left for Egypt, where he stayed until the death of Herod. And so was fulfilled what the Lord had said through the prophet: "Out of Egypt I called my son." When Herod realized that he had been outwitted by the Magi, he was furious, and he gave orders to kill all the boys in Bethlehem and its vicinity who were two years old and under, in accordance with the time he had learned from the Magi. (Matthew 2:13-16)

The Good News

The good news is that His background didn't define who He was. None of His problems, struggles or anything He went through defined who He was or who He would become. God's plan for His life was bigger than His problems.

The Truth

You were created by God. You are important to God. You are a unique, distinct, important, person and God loves you the way He made you. Your problems will not change who you are, how you are or how important you are to God!

Agreeing with God

I might as well be myself, face my problems and watch God carry out His master plan for my life!

I Agree _____

Text, Tweet, Tag or Post This

God's plan is working for my good

The master has a master plan for me

God's plan is bigger than my problems

Herod couldn't kill Jesus and the devil can't kill you either!

I am a unique, distinct, important child of God who loves me

God made me. God loves me. Too bad if you don't like me

Let's Get To Work

List one (1) thing you want to be, and two (2) things you want
to do in life. Remember to hold onto your dreams!

_____

_____

_____

Take Action

Be proud of who you are

Always introduce yourself with confidence

Hold your head up high

Speak loudly and clearly

Goal #2 - Hanging with others

The Background Story

There is a story in the bible about John the Baptist who was preaching the good news about Jesus Christ. A crowd of people had come from all over to hear John preach. After hearing John's message, many people repented of their sins and were baptized.

John the Baptist was Jesus' cousin. His job was to lead the way and tell everyone about Jesus. God had great plans for the two of them. Each one would validate the other and together they would do great things for God.

Some of the people who came to hear John were good and some were bad. The Pharisees were there. The Sadducees were there. Jesus was on the way. Jesus had a reputation already. People knew about Him before He had ever showed up. Let's read all about it!

The Bible Story

In those days John the Baptist came, preaching in the wilderness of Judea and saying, "Repent, for the kingdom of heaven has come near." This is he who was spoken of through the prophet Isaiah: "A voice of one calling in the wilderness, 'Prepare the way for the Lord, make straight paths for him.'" John's clothes were made of camel's hair, and he had a leather belt around his waist. His food was locusts and wild honey. People went out to him from Jerusalem and all Judea and the whole region of the Jordan. Confessing their sins, they were baptized by him in the Jordan River. (Matthew 3:1-6)

The Good News

Let me say it again, some people liked what they heard about Jesus and wanted to meet Him. Others did not like what they heard about Jesus. They were his enemies before they even met him (face to face). Still, nothing stopped Jesus from coming around. God did not intend for Jesus to hide out from other people. Jesus was not afraid of what others thought, felt or had to say about Him. Jesus had impeccable courage in the face of opposition. He still hung out with other people though some were His good friends and some were not.

The Truth

Some people will like you and some won't. Either way you should simply be yourself. You should be bold in your faith. Be confident and courageous in every situation. Love and enjoy your friends. Be aware of people who dislike you but treat them with genuine love and care too.

Agreeing with God

I might as well accept how God made me. My friends and I are a little different from each other but it's ok. God wants me to be unique. Unique people do unique things.

I Agree _____

Text, Tweet, Tag or Post This

Unique people do unique things

Difference makers are different kinds of people

Being me is being free - Being like Jesus gives me liberty

The Kingdom of Heaven is here –Jesus has everything you need

Let's Get To Work

List one (1) bad thing that people have said about you, and two (2) good things God thinks about you.

_____

_____

_____

Take Action

Love yourself and treat yourself great then treat others the same way

Talk about things that you like but remember to talk about things that others like too.

Goal #3 - Fitting in

The Background Story

There is a beautiful story in the bible about how God offered salvation to all people. John the Baptist has a role in this story. Jesus has a role too, a much bigger role. Let's read about how each man play's a part in God's plan of salvation.

The Bible Story

"I baptize you with water for repentance. But after me comes one who is more powerful than I, whose sandals I am not worthy to carry. He will baptize you with the Holy Spirit and fire. His winnowing fork is in his hand, and he will clear his threshing floor, gathering his wheat into the barn and burning up the chaff with unquenchable fire." (Matthew 3:11-12)

The Good News

John and Jesus are different people. They have different roles in God's plan. John could not do what Jesus was supposed to do. Jesus was not there to do what John was assigned to do. Others may not like us or what we are called to do, but that's ok. We still have a part in the story. We have a role in God's plan. Even if we are not popular, rich or famous, we are important. We all have a chance to fit in to God's plan.

Agreeing with God

I might as well accept the good and bad that God has for me. God will fit me into His plan, His team, His mission, and the victorious outcome that is waiting for me. I will accept it, join in. We are all different from each other. What I bring to the table will be so helpful. Others may not pat me on the back for it, but they will look back and appreciate what I had to offer.

I Agree _____

Text, Tweet, Tag or Post This

God will pat me on the back for my good works later

Let's Get To Work

List one (1) thing that makes you different from
others, and two (2) things that makes you special.

_____

_____

_____

Take Action

You are a representative of your family. Represent them well
Everyone is an equal part of the team. Like links on a bike
chain, or spokes on a wheel, no one is greater than the rest.
You are just as good as everyone else. Just as important.

Goal #4 - Being different

The Background Story

This is a story where God, our Father tells us about His son, Jesus. We learn that Jesus is different, very special. When Jesus was baptized, God spoke publicly and proudly about him. God said that Jesus is His son that He is proud of. This story shows us that God expects us all to follow the rules even if we are a little different.

The Bible Story

Then Jesus came from Galilee to the Jordan to be baptized by John. But John tried to deter him, saying, "I need to be baptized by you, and do you come to me?" Jesus replied, "Let it be so now; it is proper for us to do this to fulfill all righteousness." Then John consented. As soon as Jesus was baptized, he went up out of the water. At that moment heaven was opened, and he saw the Spirit of God descending like a dove and alighting on him. And a voice from heaven said, "This is my Son, whom I love; with him I am well pleased." (Matthew 3:13-17)

Agreeing with God

I might as well accept that I will be used to set an example. Where there are rules, I have to follow them and show others how to do the same. My parents, guardians and loved ones will celebrate me for it. My God will smile on me and continue to use me to show others the way. That is the price I pay for being loved. Love makes me different.

I Agree _____

Text, Tweet, Tag or Post This

Love makes me different

Let's Get To Work

List one (1) rule you hate to follow, and two (2) rules you follow that pleases your parents, teachers, or God.

Part 1 Action Plan for discovering who you are

Be proud of who you are.

State your name loud & proud, clearly

Always introduce yourself with confidence

You're a representative of your family. Represent them well

Be a team player, an equal part of the team

Be yourself; you're as good and important as everyone else

Be smart, strong, beautiful, and amazing

Be proud of your family, name, background, and heritage

Part 2 – Getting Along with Others
(In the Crowd)

Are you a square peg trying to fit into a round hole? Do you want to fit in with other people? Do other kids dislike you for no reason? Do you seem different from the rest? Do you feel like you are living a life that was meant for someone else to live? Do you feel that you should be liked and treated better? Let's look at how to get along with the people we live, and learn with. We will master getting along with others.

Goal #5 - Facing bullies

The Background Story

Before Jesus started His ministry, He was tempted by the devil in the Wilderness. His temptation came when He was most vulnerable. He was on a 40 day fast. During these 40 days, Jesus would abstain from eating, or other activities and replace them with spiritual activities to help Him experience or depend on God. During this period of time, He chose not to give in to the temptation of the devil. Jesus relied on the word of God and defeated His bully. Let's read about how Jesus faced his bully.

The Bible Story

Then Jesus was led by the Spirit into the wilderness to be tempted by the devil. After fasting forty days and forty nights, he was hungry. The tempter came to him and said, "If you are the Son of God, tell these stones to become bread." Jesus answered, "It is written: 'Man shall not live on bread alone, but on every word that comes from the mouth of God.'" Then the devil took him to the holy city and had him stand on the highest point of the temple. "If you are the Son of God," he said, "throw yourself down. For it is written: '"He will command his angels concerning you, and they will lift you up in their hands, so that you will not strike your foot against a stone."' Jesus answered him, "It is also written: 'Do not put the Lord your God to the test.'"

Again, the devil took him to a very high mountain and showed him all the kingdoms of the world and their splendor. "All this I will give you," he said, "if you will bow down and worship me." Jesus said to him, "Away from me, Satan! For it is written: 'Worship the Lord your God, and serve him only.'" Then the devil left him, and angels came and attended him. (Matthew 4:1-11)

Agreeing with God

I will accept it. Bullies want to intimidate me, trick me, and ruin my name while making a name for themselves. I won't fall for it. My name is already worth more than all of the money in the world. I won't ruin it by letting bullies control me. I am in control of my own actions.

I Agree _____

Text, Tweet, Tag or Post This

I am in control of me. God gave the authority!

I have God's permission to be strong!

Let's Get To Work

List one (1) bully in your life and two (2) things from God that can help you to stand up to bullies

Goal #6 - Standing up for myself

The Background Story

Even though they arrested John and put him in prison, Jesus still lived the life He was supposed to live. He still did what he was supposed to do. For Jesus, that meant he was supposed to preach. Now, God wants you to live the life He has planned for you.

God has a purpose for you, and basic instructions for you to live by. God wants you live for Him each day regardless of what others have to say about you, and regardless of how they treat you. Sometimes you will have to stand up for yourself to others. Sometimes you have to continue doing what you are supposed to do, right in their faces. Doing right pleases God and disappoints others. You must live to please God, even if it hurts others and makes them angry. The benefit that you have is that you are living for God and are doing what pleases Him, so God will have your back. God will give you strength when you need it. God will help you make friends when you need it and God will encourage you.

The Bible Story

When Jesus heard that John had been put in prison, he withdrew to Galilee. Leaving Nazareth, he went and lived in Capernaum. From that time on Jesus began to preach, "Repent, for the kingdom of heaven has come near." (Matthew 4:12-13, 17)

Agreeing with God

I will just accept it, life will be great when I stand up for myself and do what I am called to do. I will shatter the expectations of others when I do what's right.

I Agree _____

Text, Tweet, Tag or Post This

I am obediently shattering expectations

Goal #7 - Making friends

The Background Story

Jesus meets several new friends, Peter and Andrew, James and John. Jesus knew that these friendships would be close. They were all working as fishermen. Jesus knew that fishing was important to them, but their friendship would lead to new experiences. They would discover something more important than their jobs as fishermen.

The Bible Story

As Jesus was walking beside the Sea of Galilee, he saw two brothers, Simon called Peter and his brother Andrew. They were casting a net into the lake, for they were fishermen. "Come, follow me," Jesus said, "and I will send you out to fish for people." At once they left their nets and followed him. Going on from there, he saw two other brothers, James son of Zebedee and his brother John. They were in a boat with their father Zebedee, preparing their nets. Jesus called them, and immediately they left the boat and their father and followed him. (Matthew 4:18-22)

Agreeing with God

I might as well accept it. At some point I must make new friends. We will have different backgrounds, interests, hobbies, careers and personalities. It's ok that we are different. When my new friends see what is special about me, they will support me and I will support them too. This is a part of being in a relationship together and we are worth it.

I Agree _____

Text, Tweet, Tag or Post This

I'm making new friends. We're all worth it

Let's Get To Work

List one (1) friend, one (1) thing you have in common.

_____

_____

_____

Now list one (1) thing that others should like about you.

_____

_____

_____

Goal #8 – Mingling with the crowd

The Background Story

Jesus went where the crowds were. He really didn't fit into the crowd. He was in the crowd but He knew He belonged to God. He learned about the people in the crowd. He taught, preached and healed the people in the crowd. Eventually the crowd followed Him wherever He went.

The Bible Story

Jesus went throughout Galilee, teaching in their synagogues, proclaiming the good news of the kingdom, and healing every disease and sickness among the people. News about him spread all over Syria, and people brought to him all who were ill with various diseases, those suffering severe pain, the demon-possessed, those having seizures, and the paralyzed; and he healed them. Large crowds from Galilee, the Decapolis, Jerusalem, Judea and the region across the Jordan followed him (Matthew 4:23-25)

The Good News

The Good news is that Jesus was available to everyone in the crowd.

Agreeing with God

You might as well accept it. You have gifts, abilities, skills, talents, character and qualities that will help others. Now that you know who you are, and that you are able to get along with others, you can and will reengage the crowd of people with a mission and a motive to help them. You will humbly and quietly bless the crowd with your presence. Be a blessing to others. Have confidence in what you have to offer.

I Agree _____

Let's Get To Work

List two (2) gifts, talents, qualities, or character traits that you possess that you can use to do good things and be a blessing to others.

_____

_____

_____

_____

_____

_____

Goal #9 - Understanding the crowd

The Background Story

Jesus was hanging out at Matthew's house with the crowd. There were a lot of people at the house. Jesus' friends, the disciples were there with him. The Pharisees were there. They had evil in their hearts and they were mean toward Jesus. They were other people there that the Pharisees called sinners. Jesus was there to make friends with the sinners. He wanted to spend time with them and teach them how to get to know God. The Pharisees picked on the disciples and they looked down on Jesus' new friends, the sinners. Jesus understood the crowd. Jesus knew that there are always people in the crowd that believed they were better than the others. Jesus was not looking to befriend the self-righteous, unkind Pharisees who disliked Jesus. Instead, he wanted to befriend the sinners, who would appreciate Jesus' help.

The Bible Story

While Jesus was having dinner at Matthew's house, many tax collectors and sinners came and ate with him and his disciples. When the Pharisees saw this, they asked his disciples, "Why does your teacher eat with tax collectors and sinners?" On hearing this, Jesus said, "It is not the healthy who need a doctor, but the sick. But go and learn what this means: 'I desire mercy, not sacrifice.' For I have not come to call the righteous, but sinners." (Matthew 4:9-13)

Agreeing with God

You might as well accept that there are both friends and enemies in the crowd. There are different types of people in the crowd. There are people who will love you and want to be friends with you, there are people who will appreciate you and welcome you and then there are people who will resent you and want you to go away. You must accept all three (3) before you can identify them and then appreciate them.

I Agree _____

Let's Get To Work

List one friend you are thankful for, one person you want to become friends with, and one person who is not a friend but you would like to learn from them. Now, go tell each of them!

_____

_____

_____

Goal #10 - Joining a team

The Background Story

One day Jesus was traveling with the disciples, teaching bout the kingdom of God. Jesus stopped to teach his disciples a very important lesson that the harvest is plentiful but the workers are few.

Jesus knew that it was an important time in history for the people of the Jewish faith. Many people were ready to repent of their sins. They were beginning to believe in the Son of God who would take away their sins and introduce them to the father. Jesus needed people who would join the team and help recruit new believers.

The Bible Story

Jesus went through all the towns and villages, teaching in their synagogues, proclaiming the good news of the kingdom and healing every disease and sickness. When he saw the crowds, he had compassion on them, because they were harassed and helpless, like sheep without a shepherd. Then he said to his disciples, "The harvest is plentiful but the workers are few. Ask the Lord of the harvest, therefore, to send out workers into his harvest field." (Matthew 4:35-38)

The Good News

The good news is that Jesus was committed to doing God's work. He prayed for more workers. If you are a believer, then join His team. He will change your life.

Agreeing with God

Just accept it. Sometimes you will encounter groups of people, teams and small circles of friends who will ask you to join them. When you find the right fit, join in, have fun, get the job done, but most importantly, learn to be a team player.

I Agree _____

Let's Get To Work

List three (3) teams (groups) you admire. What would you do if you were on the team? How would you be helpful?

_____

_____

_____

_____

_____

Part 2 Action Plan

The kids you see, in your class, and neighborhood are your future friends and buddies. You will get to know some of them, like some, grow up with them and have memories of fun times that you will hold onto forever.

- Accept your friends for who they are.

- Be yourself and let them accept you too.

- Be nice, play nice.

- Take turns talking.

- Take turns taking the lead.

- Take turns having the fun part in a game.

- Always be respectful of others.

- Don't single anyone out for being different

- Don't embarrass others for seeing things differently.

- Be patient and kind with others.

- Help others.

- Help do the hard work now and have fun with your team later

Part 3 – Taking Authority

(Leading the Crowd)

Goal #11 - Taking the lead

The Background Story

In Matthew chapter 10, Jesus gives the twelve disciples authority to go out and help people by healing them and restoring their quality of life. While they were doing good things for others, Jesus knew that there would be some mean people around so Jesus taught them to be smart and not to pick up bad behaviors like others. He told them not to be afraid of the others, and to keep on doing the good things they were supposed to do.

Jesus was being a leader for the disciples. There will be times when you will have to step up and be a leader.

The Bible Story

Jesus called his twelve disciples to him and gave them authority to drive out impure spirits and to heal every disease and sickness. These twelve Jesus sent out with the following instructions: "Do not go among the Gentiles or enter any town of the Samaritans. Go rather to the lost sheep of Israel. As you go, proclaim this message: 'The kingdom of heaven has come near.' Heal the sick, raise the dead, cleanse those who have leprosy, drive out demons. Freely you have received; freely give. "I am sending you out like sheep among wolves. Therefore be as shrewd as snakes and as innocent as doves. Be on your guard; you will be handed over to the local councils and be flogged in the synagogues. On my account you will be brought before governors and kings as witnesses to them and to the Gentiles. But when they arrest you, do not worry about what to say or how to say it. At that time you will be given what to say, for it will not be you speaking, but the Spirit of your Father speaking through you. (Matthew 10:1, 5-8, 16-20)

Agreeing with God

Just accept it. You will to do what's right even when no one else is willing to. Then you will have to show others the way so they can do the right thing as well. That's leadership. Taking authority for your own life and the decisions you make is leadership. Leaders help others and stand up for what's right.

I Agree _____

Take a break and pray

May God develops you into a strong leader

Goal #12 - Doing what's right

The Background Story

This is a remarkable story about how Jesus forgives and heals a Paralyzed Man. Jesus has the love and compassion of the almighty father living in his heart, so Jesus would be easily moved with compassion whenever he saw someone else hurting. In this story, a man was paralyzed, and his friends had enough faith to take him to get healed. Jesus knew he could help the man. Jesus had the authority of our father in heaven to forgive the man's sins and heal him. Jesus did both. The crowd was excited, but there were people in the crowd who were evil. They confronted Jesus for doing what's right. Jesus confronted them about their evil thoughts and went back to helping the paralyzed man. One kind gesture by Jesus helped the man become restored, able to live healthy, happy, and whole.

The Bible Story

Jesus stepped into a boat, crossed over and came to his own town. Some men brought to him a paralyzed man, lying on a mat. When Jesus saw their faith, he said to the man, "Take heart, son; your sins are forgiven." At this, some of the teachers of the law said to themselves, "This fellow is blaspheming!" Knowing their thoughts, Jesus said, "Why do you entertain evil thoughts in your hearts? Which is easier: to say, 'Your sins are forgiven,' or to say, 'Get up and walk'? But I want you to know that the Son of Man has authority on earth to forgive sins." So he said to the paralyzed man, "Get up, take your mat and go home." Then the man got up and went home. When the crowd saw this, they were filled with awe; and they praised God, who had given such authority to man. Matthew 9:1-8)

The Good News

The good news is that Jesus came to restore every one of us to a relationship with God and to heal every one of our lives. God wants us to be healthy, happy, and whole.

Agreeing with God

Just accept it. You will have opportunities to help other people become smarter, stronger, happier, more faithful and more fun. Some people will talk about you and your methods but God created you to recognize evil but still do what it right. Accept the challenge and run with it. Others will be blessed by God working through you.

I Agree _____

Text, Tweet, Tag or Post This

God blesses others through me

Take a break and pray

Pray that God gives you the courage and integrity to always do what is right. Others may laugh at you or tease you, but it is worth being teased if God is proud of you.
It's worth it if God is pleased with your courage.

Part 4 – Keeping the Faith

(When the Crowd fights back)

Goal #13 - Believing I can do it

The Background Story

The twelve disciples are sent on a dangerous mission. They have the same authority over impure spirits, diseases and sickness that Jesus has. They would be treated meanly by important people. Jesus told them not to worry because God will be with them, speaking through them.

I offer the same advice to you. Wherever God sends you, remember that God loves you, God believes in you, and God will help you. Though you will be treated meanly by others, do not be afraid. God expects you to have faith in Him. Know that God will speak through you when it is time to speak. God will work through you when it is time to work.

The Bible Story

Jesus called his twelve disciples to him and gave them authority to drive out impure spirits and to heal every disease and sickness. "I am sending you out like sheep among wolves. Therefore be as shrewd as snakes and as innocent as doves. Be on your guard; you will be handed over to the local councils and be flogged in the synagogues. On my account you will be brought before governors and kings as witnesses to them and to the Gentiles. But when they arrest you, do not worry about what to say or how to say it. At that time you will be given what to say, for it will not be you speaking, but the Spirit of your Father speaking through you. (Matthew 10:1, 16-20)

Agreeing with God

I might as well accept it. God has created me to do great things and I can only accomplish them if I believe that I can do them. As I begin each day, I will remember the authority that God has given me. I will remember the great things God has set before me, and I will remember that I can do them!

I Agree _____

Text, Tweet, Tag or Post This

Jesus is with me so I can do whatever God says

Take a break and pray

Pray for strong faith then use it.
One day you will look back and see that by faith, you obeyed God and did great things

Goal #14 - Being Bold with Stubborn People

The Background Story

Jesus knew that the evil people in the crowd hated him. Jesus told his friends that just like he was hated, they will be hated as well. Jesus' advice to them was to be bold. Don't be afraid of people because only God deserves to be feared. Though people can hurt or even kill you, you should not fear them. Only God is worth it. His wrath, and eternal judgment is even worse. Treat men as men the way they should be treated. They should be loved, respected and honored but not feared. Continue to be bold for God, even when you are confronted by scary people.

The Bible Story

"The student is not above the teacher, nor a servant above his master. It is enough for students to be like their teachers, and servants like their masters. "So do not be afraid of them, for there is nothing concealed that will not be disclosed, or hidden that will not be made known. What I tell you in the dark, speak in the daylight; what is whispered in your ear, proclaim from the roofs. Do not be afraid of those who kill the body but cannot kill the soul. Rather, be afraid of the One who can destroy both soul and body in hell. Are not two sparrows sold for a penny? Yet not one of them will fall to the ground outside your Father's care. And even the very hairs of your head are all numbered. So don't be afraid; you are worth more than many sparrows. (Matthew 10:24-31)

Agreeing with God

I might as well accept it. I am fearfully and wonderfully made. I was created to be virtuous, valiant, bold, regal, powerful and awe-inspiring, like the God who made me.

God is trying to teach me how to be bold. God wants me to maintain my composure and confidence. Even scary and powerful people cannot take away what God has put in me.

I Agree _____

Text, Tweet, Tag or Post This

I'm confident and cool, fearfully & wonderfully made

Take a break and pray

Pray that you're not overconfident, but not underestimated either. Then pray you see others with a heart of love, not fear.

Goal #15 - Being Confident of my work

The Background Story

John was a dear friend of Jesus. One day he heard stories about Jesus. He wasn't sure if Jesus was the person that he thought Jesus was, but Jesus was confident in who he was, how he was supposed to act and what he was supposed to do.

There will be times when others don't believe in you. They will doubt you. They will tease you about what you do, but you must trust God. God is working through you. God can do immeasurably more than all we ask or imagine, according to his power that is at work within us.

The Bible Story

After Jesus had finished instructing his twelve disciples, he went on from there to teach and preach in the towns of Galilee. When John, who was in prison, heard about the deeds of the Messiah, he sent his disciples to ask him, "Are you the one who is to come, or should we expect someone else?" Jesus replied, "Go back and report to John what you hear and see: The blind receive sight, the lame walk, those who have leprosy are cleansed, the deaf hear, the dead are raised, and the good news is proclaimed to the poor. Blessed is anyone who does not stumble on account of me." (Matthew 11:1-6)

Agreeing with God

I might as well accept it. When others doubt me, God expects me to have confidence in what I am doing. God wants me to keep going. In the end, I will be glad that I did not quit.

I Agree _____

Text, Tweet, Tag or Post This

I won't quit. I'm all in with Jesus

Take a break and pray

Take a break and pray that you will be cool, confident and relaxed in any situation, in everything you do, and even if the worst possible thing(s) in the world happened to you.

Goal #16 - Finishing the job

The Background Story

The crucifixion of Jesus is the most saddening scene in all scripture. The soldiers mocked Jesus. They spit on him and called him names. Then they led him away and tortured him by crucifying him on the cross. Being crucified was humiliating and painful but Jesus did not come down from the cross. He stayed on the cross. On one hand, he endured the humiliation of people and on the other hand, he fulfilled the plan of God.

When the crowd sees you doing your best to do what is right, the crowd will respond with either praise or envy. When you are achieving great things for God, the crowd will mock you as it did to Jesus. People will laugh at you, talk about you and call you names. People will hurt your feelings and make you wish you could simply disappear. You may feel embarrassed. You may even cry. You may want to end your own life to end the pain and humiliation you feel, but that is not what God wants you to do. God wants you to finish the job! There is life beyond the pain! It gets better later. After this, you will arrive at a better place. You will become the person that God had in mind for you to become. You needed the right set of painful circumstances to feed your strength.

The Bible Story

Then the governor's soldiers took Jesus into the Praetorium and gathered the whole company of soldiers around him. They stripped him and put a scarlet robe on him, and then twisted together a crown of thorns and set it on his head. They put a staff in his right hand. Then they knelt in front of him and mocked him. "Hail, king of the Jews!" they said. They spit on him, and took the staff and struck him on the head again and again. After they had mocked him, they took off the robe and put his own clothes on him. Then they led him away to crucify him. (Matthew 27:27-31)

Agreeing with God

I might as well accept it. God is not finished with me yet. I will finish my part and become a finished product. God sees a vintage me that cannot be imitated or recreated.

I Agree _____

Text, Tweet, Tag or Post This

I am a vintage model, a child of God, created by God!

Take a break and pray

Pray for the will to obey, the courage to hang in there, and the victory to stand tall in the end

Part 5 – Treating Others Right

(When the crowd starts listening to me)

Goal #17 – Broadening my Circle

The Background Story

Here is a story about two blind men who heard the crowd pass by. They needed a miracle and knew the only person that could perform the miracle and restore their sight was in the crowd, leading the way. What happened when they asked for help? How did the crowd respond? How did Jesus respond? How should we treat a stranger who needs our help? How hard or easy is it to make new friends? How do we act when we are the in crowd, the popular ones, with special gifts and abilities and are in position to help someone else? Have you ever been in the spotlight, or in a position of authority, where all of the attention was on you, and you gave it up just long enough to help someone else? Trust me, and try it. It's worth it!

The Bible Story

As Jesus and his disciples were leaving Jericho, a large crowd followed him. Two blind men were sitting by the roadside, and when they heard that Jesus was going by, they shouted, "Lord, Son of David, have mercy on us!" The crowd rebuked them and told them to be quiet, but they shouted all the louder, "Lord, Son of David, have mercy on us!" Jesus stopped and called them. "What do you want me to do for you?" he asked. "Lord," they answered, "we want our sight." Jesus had compassion on them and touched their eyes. Immediately they received their sight and followed him. (Matthew 20:29-34)

The Good News

The good news is that God moves me into position with popular, important, ingenious, innovative and wealthy people for a reason. God helps me establish relationships with people who are affluent so we can share love, prosperity, authority, and power with one another. The people that I welcome into friendship and fellowship will help me get to where God wants people that I don't want to deal with.

Agreeing with God

I might as well accept it. God wants to know how I will treat a stranger who needs my help. Will I hide in the crowd and let the crowd mistreat them or will I stand up and be a blessing to them? God is watching and waiting for me to decide, so I agree to broaden my circle with new friends. I will be a blessing to others.

I Agree _____

Text, Tweet, Tag or Post This

I'm being me, getting along, taking authority and keeping the faith

Take a break and pray

Now pray for others. Pray that others can learn from Jesus so they can become like Jesus Christ, able to get along with others, to take authority, and to keep the faith.

Journey of Faith Ministries

ABOUT THE AUTHOR

Dr. Derrick L Randolph, Sr. is from Baltimore, Maryland.